EASIEST
KEYBOARD
COLLECTION

Swing

WISE PUBLICATIONS
London/New York/Paris/Sydney/Copenhagen/Madrid/Tokyo

Exclusive Distributors:

Music Sales Limited
8/9 Frith Street,
London W1V 5TZ, England.

Music Sales Pty Limited
120 Rothschild Avenue,
Rosebery, NSW 2018,
Australia.

Order No. AM959101
ISBN 0-7119-7971-5
This book © Copyright 1999 by Wise Publications

Book design by Chloë Alexander
Compiled by Nick Crispin
Music arranged by Roger Day
Music processed by Paul Ewers Music Design

Printed in the United Kingdom by
Caligraving Limited, Thetford, Norfolk.

Cover photograph courtesy of Corbis

Your Guarantee of Quality
As publishers, we strive to produce every book to the highest
commercial standards.
The music has been freshly engraved and the book has been carefully
designed to minimise awkward page turns and to make playing from
it a real pleasure.
Particular care has been given to specifying acid-free, neutral-sized
paper made from pulps which have not been elemental chlorine
bleached. This pulp is from farmed sustainable forests and was
produced with special regard for the environment.
Throughout, the printing and binding have been planned to ensure
a sturdy, attractive publication which should give years of enjoyment.
If your copy fails to meet our high standards, please inform us and
we will gladly replace it.

Music Sales' complete catalogue describes thousands of titles and is
available in full colour sections by subject, direct from Music Sales
Limited. Please state your areas of interest and send a cheque/postal
order for £1.50 for postage to: Music Sales Limited, Newmarket Road,
Bury St. Edmunds, Suffolk IP33 3YB.

www.musicsales.co.uk

Contents

AIN'T NOBODY HERE BUT US CHICKENS

Words & Music by Joan Whitney & Alex Kramer
© Copyright 1947 Pickwick Music Corporation, USA.
Universal/MCA Music Limited, 77 Fulham Palace Road, London W6.
All Rights Reserved. International Copyright Secured.

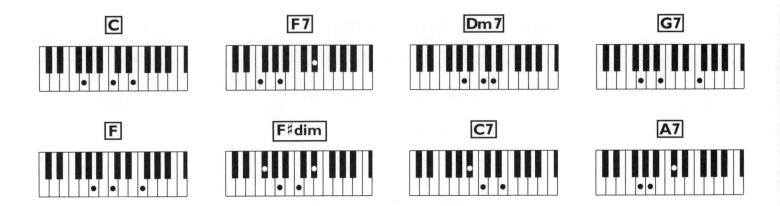

Voice: **Jazz Guitar**
Rhythm: **Cool**
Tempo: ♩ = 124

There ain't no-bo-dy here but us chick-ens, there ain't no-bo-dy here at all____ so____

quiet your-self____ and stop that fuss,____ there ain't no-bo-dy here but us.____ We chick-ens

tryin' to sleep____ and you butt in____ and hob-ble, hob-ble, hob-ble, hob-ble, it's a sin.____

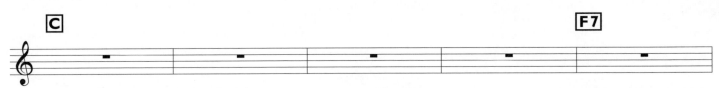

(Spoken:) Now farmer Brown lit his corned cob pipe, he looked down at his trusty dog and he said "Hey, if the chickens say they alright,

they are alright. Let's head back to the shack, Jack." But the dog wasn't convinced, he said "Go back to the henhouse"

gave a little doggy knock, and in his best chickenese said "Is everything alright?" I said there

ain't no-bo-dy here but us chick-ens, there ain't no-bo-dy here at all.___ So___

stop that fuss___ and rais-in' dust,___ there ain't no-bo-dy here but us.___ So kind-ly

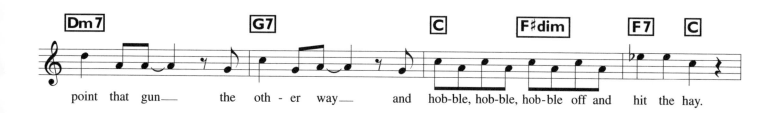

point that gun___ the oth-er way___ and hob-ble, hob-ble, hob-ble off and hit the hay.

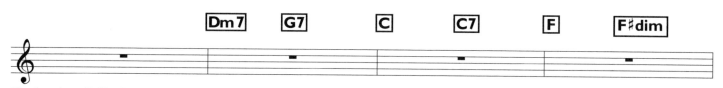

(Spoken:) O.K. I guess you're right. I'm off to sleep. Goodnight. Hey, boss man, what d'you think?

Ea - sy pick-in's, ain't no-bo-dy here but us chick-ens.___

BEAT ME DADDY, EIGHT TO THE BAR

Words & Music Don Raye, Hughie Prince & Eleanor Sheehy

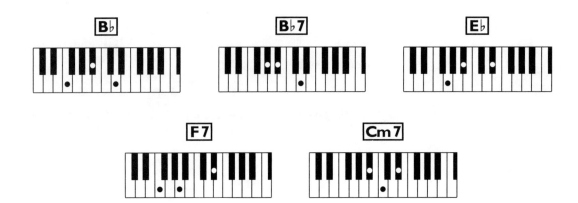

Voice: **Clarinet**

Rhythm: **Swing**

Tempo: ♩ = 118

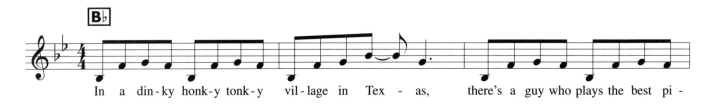

In a din-ky honk-y tonk-y vil-lage in Tex - as, there's a guy who plays the best pi -

-a - no by far,___ he can play pi - a - no a - ny way that you like___ it,

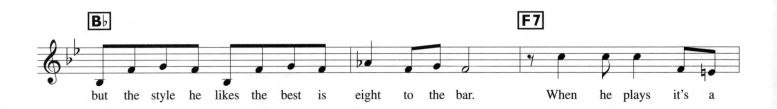

but the style he likes the best is eight to the bar. When he plays it's a

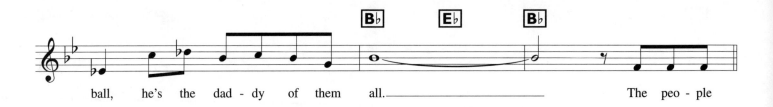

ball, he's the dad - dy of them all._____ The peo - ple

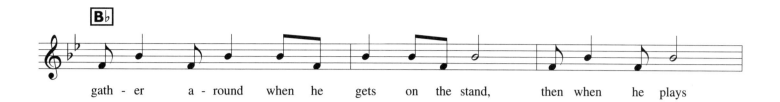

gath - er a - round when he gets on the stand, then when he plays

he gets a hand. The rhy - thm he beats puts the cats in a trance,

no - bo - dy there both - ers to dance. But when he jams with the bass and gui - tar._

_ They hol - ler "Aw beat me, dad - dy, eight to the bar."_ A

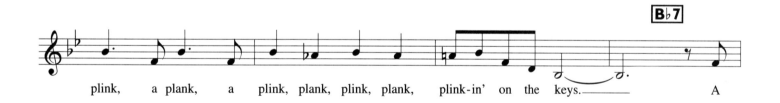

plink, a plank, a plink, plank, plink, plank, plink-in' on the keys._ A

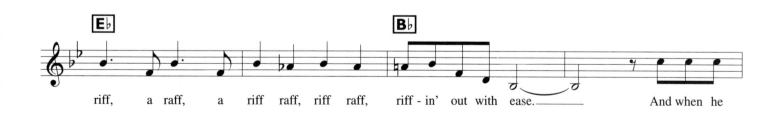

riff, a raff, a riff raff, riff raff, riff - in' out with ease._ And when he

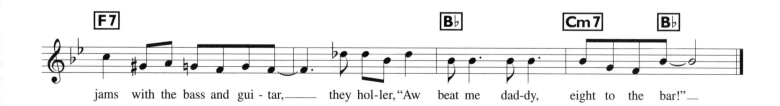

jams with the bass and gui - tar,_ they hol - ler, "Aw beat me dad-dy, eight to the bar!"_

7

FLYING HOME

By Benny Goodman & Lionel Hampton

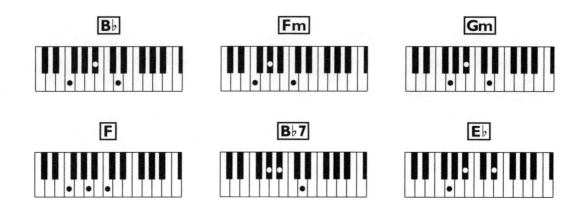

Voice: **Piano 1**

Rhythm: **Swing**

Tempo: ♩ = 108

HEY! BA-BA-RE-BOP

Words & Music by Lionel Hampton & Curley Hammer

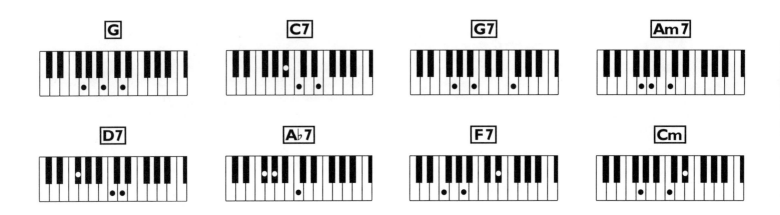

Voice: **Clarinet**

Rhythm: **Big Band**

Tempo: ♩ = 128

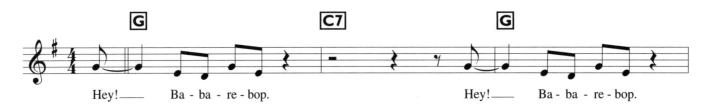

Hey!— Ba - ba - re - bop.   Hey!— Ba - ba - re - bop.

Hey!— Ba - ba - re - bop.   Hey!—

— Ba - ba - re - bop.   Hey!— Ba - ba - re - bop.

Yes,— your ba - by knows.—   Ma -

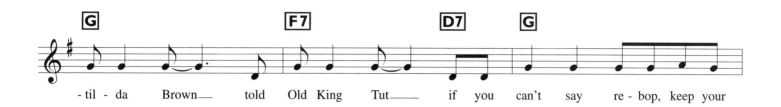

-til - da Brown___ told Old King Tut___ if you can't say re - bop, keep your

big mouth shut,___ sing - ing Hey! Ba - ba - re - bop. Hey!_

___ Ba - ba - re - bop. Hey!___ Ba - ba - re - bop. Yes,_

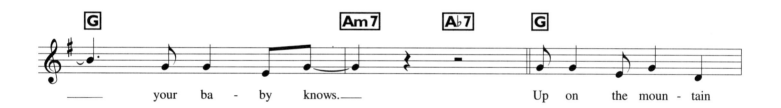

___ your ba - by knows.___ Up on the moun - tain

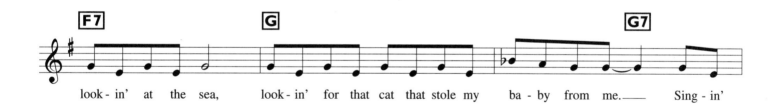

look - in' at the sea, look - in' for that cat that stole my ba - by from me.___ Sing - in'

Hey! Ba - ba - re - bop. Hey!___ Ba - ba - re - bop. Hey!_

___ Ba - ba - re - bop. Yes,___ your ba - by knows.___

HIT THAT JIVE JACK

Words & Music by John Alston & Campbell "Skeets" Tolbert

© Copyright 1941 MCA Music Publishing (a division of Universal Studios Incorporated, USA).
Universal/MCA Music Limited, 77 Fulham Palace Road, London W6.
All Rights Reserved. International Copyright Secured.

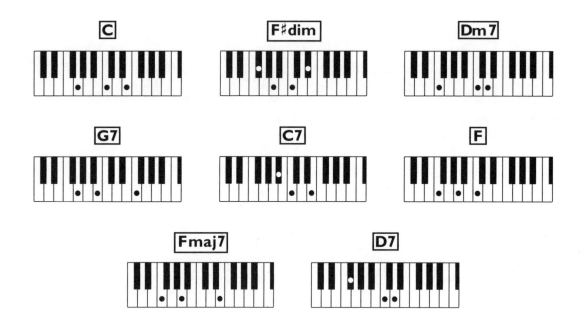

Voice: **Brass Ensemble**

Rhythm: **Swing**

Tempo: ♩ = 134

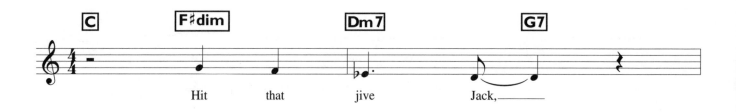

Hit that jive Jack,

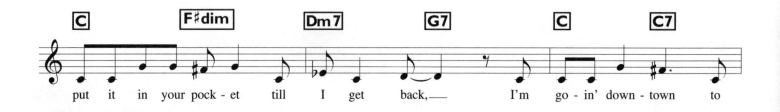

put it in your pock-et till I get back,— I'm go-in' down-town to

see a man— and I ain't got time to shake your hand.—

I WAN'NA BE LIKE YOU
(from Walt Disney Pictures' "The Jungle Book")

Words & Music by Richard M. Sherman & Robert B. Sherman

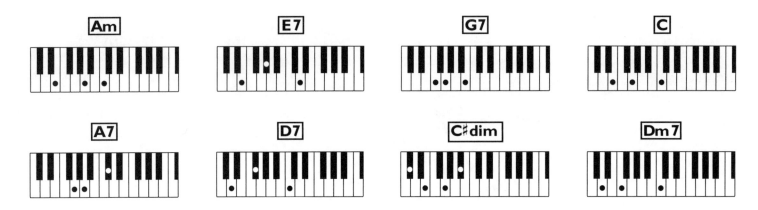

Voice: **Synth Brass 3**

Rhythm: **Big Band**

Tempo: ♩ = 136

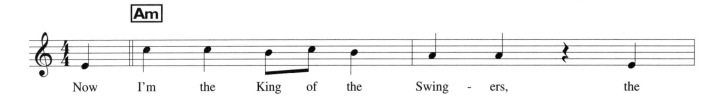

Now I'm the King of the Swing - ers, the

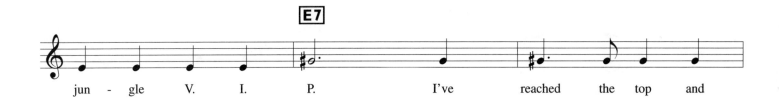

jun - gle V. I. P. I've reached the top and

had to stop and that's what's both - er - in' me. I

wan - na be a man, man - cub, and stroll right in - to

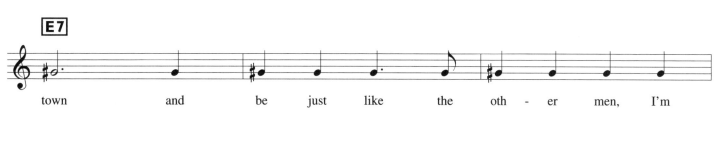

town and be just like the oth - er men, I'm

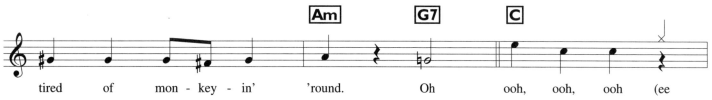

tired of mon - key - in' 'round. Oh ooh, ooh, ooh (ee

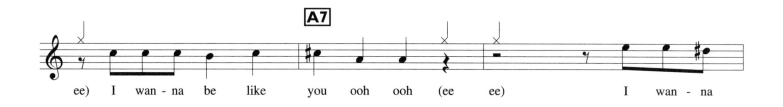

ee) I wan - na be like you ooh ooh (ee ee) I wan - na

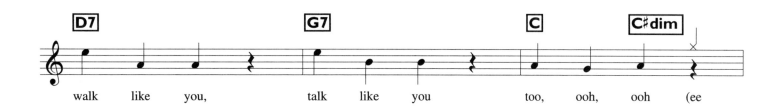

walk like you, talk like you too, ooh, ooh (ee

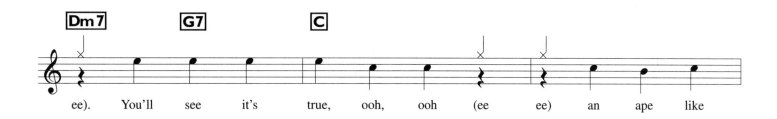

ee). You'll see it's true, ooh, ooh (ee ee) an ape like

me, ee ee (ooh ooh) can learn to be

-hu - ooh - ooh-man too, ooh, ooh (ee ee) ooh, ooh.

I'M GETTING SENTIMENTAL OVER YOU

Words by Ned Washington
Music by George Bassman

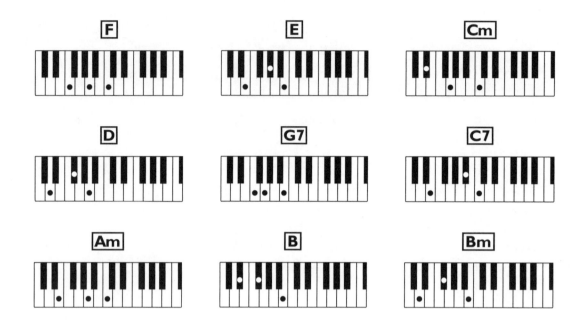

Voice: **Trumpet**

Rhythm: **Slow Swing**

Tempo: ♩ = 100

Nev - er thought I'd fall but now I hear love call, I'm

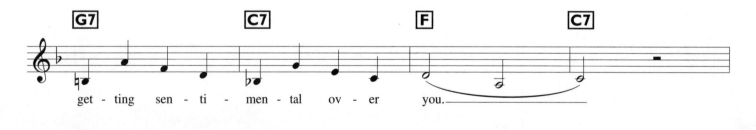

get - ting sen - ti - men - tal ov - er you.———

Things you say and do just thrill me through and through, I'm

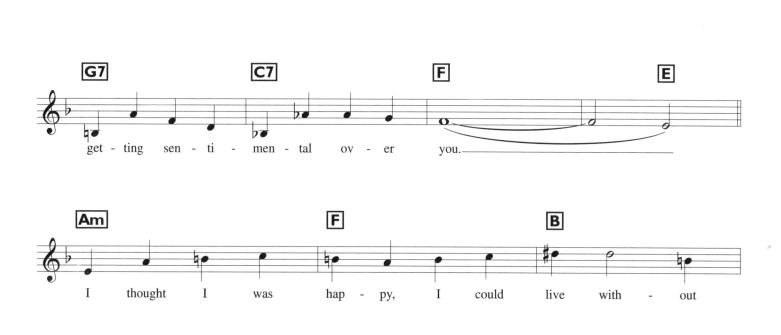

get - ting sen - ti - men - tal ov - er you. _____

I thought I was hap - py, I could live with - out

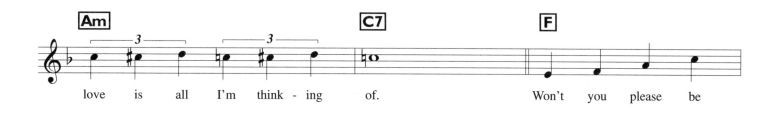

love, now I must ad - mit, that

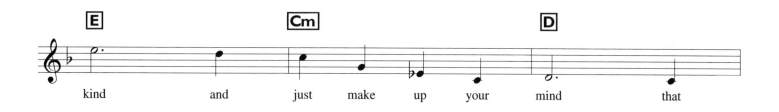

love is all I'm think - ing of. Won't you please be

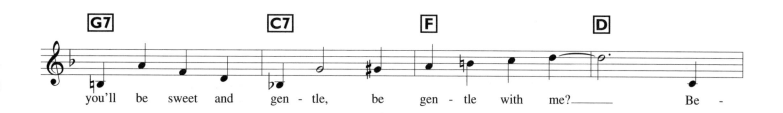

kind and just make up your mind that

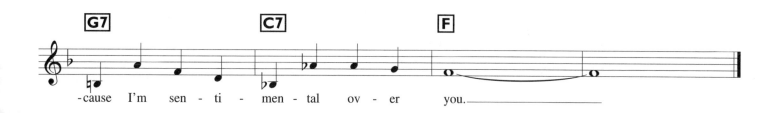

you'll be sweet and gen - tle, be gen - tle with me? _____ Be -

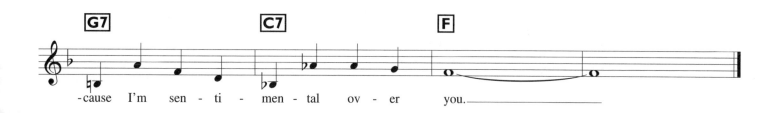

-cause I'm sen - ti - men - tal ov - er you. _____

IF YOU CAN'T SING IT
(YOU'LL HAVE TO SWING IT)

Words & Music by Sam Coslow

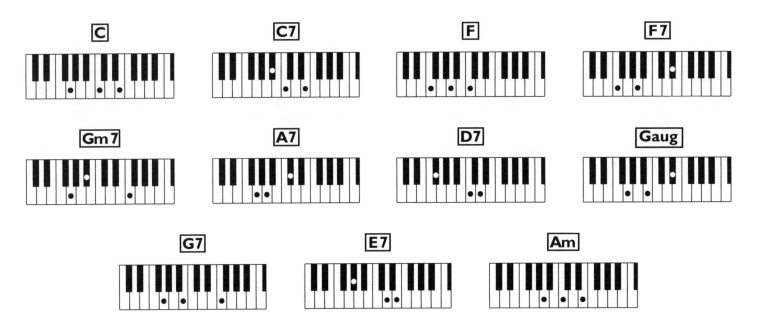

Voice: **Clarinet**

Rhythm: **Swing**

Tempo: ♩ = 118

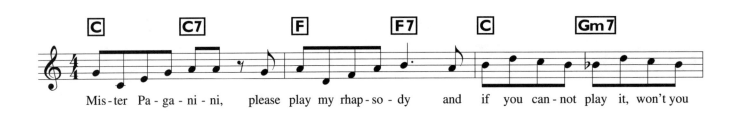

Mis-ter Pa-ga-ni-ni, please play my rhap-so-dy and if you can-not play it, won't you

sing it, and if you can't sing it you'll sim-ply have to

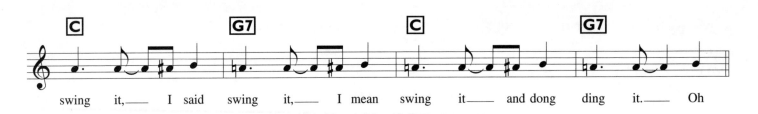

swing it,___ I said swing it,___ I mean swing it___ and dong ding it.___ Oh

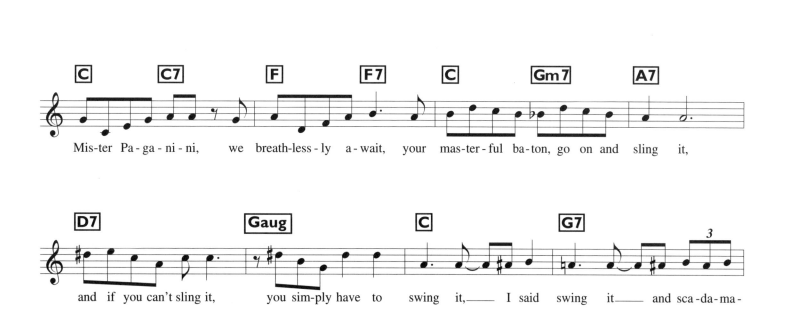

Mis-ter Pa - ga - ni - ni, we breath-less - ly a-wait, your mas-ter-ful ba-ton, go on and sling it,

and if you can't sling it, you sim-ply have to swing it,___ I said swing it___ and sca-da-ma-

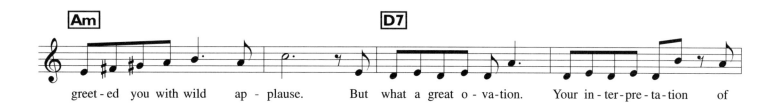

-fa___ and fa - da - ma - sca. We've heard your re - per-toire and at the fi - nal bar, we

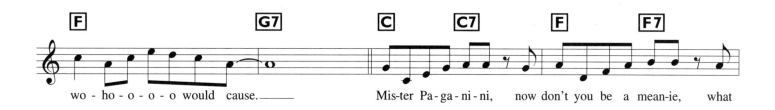

greet-ed you with wild ap - plause. But what a great o - va-tion. Your in - ter-pre-ta-tion of

wo - ho - o - o - o would cause.___ Mis-ter Pa - ga - ni - ni, now don't you be a mean-ie, what

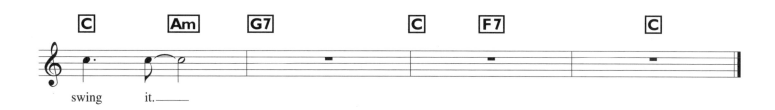

have you up your sleeve, come on and spring it, and if you don't spring it, that means you'll have to

swing it.___

IS YOU IS OR IS YOU AIN'T MY BABY?

Words & Music by Billy Austin & Louis Jordan

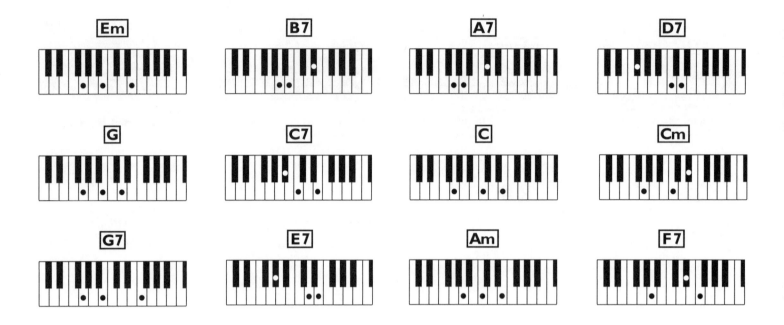

Voice: **Vibes**

Rhythm: **Swing**

Tempo: ♩= 140

Is you is, or is you ain't my ba - by?

The way you're act - ing late - ly makes me doubt.—

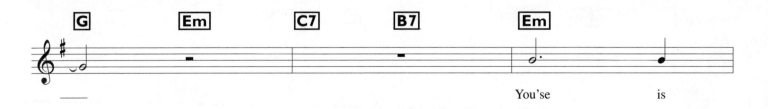

_____ You'se is

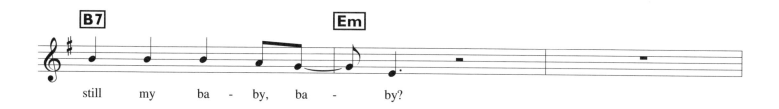

still my ba - by, ba - by?

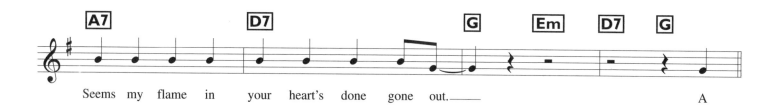

Seems my flame in your heart's done gone out._____ A

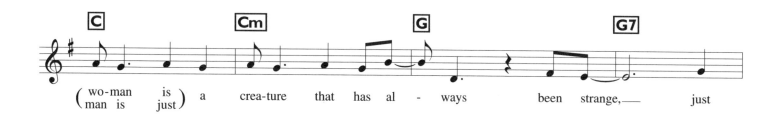

(wo-man is / man is just) a crea-ture that has al - ways been strange,_____ just

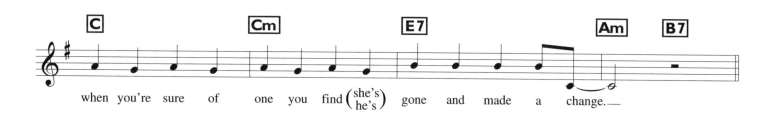

when you're sure of one you find (she's / he's) gone and made a change._____

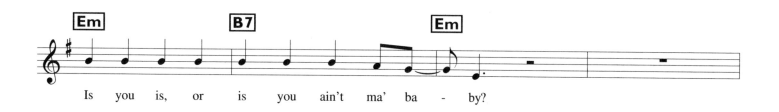

Is you is, or is you ain't ma' ba - by?

May - be ba - by's found some - bo - dy new._____ Or

is ma' ba - by still ma' ba - by true?_____

IT DON'T MEAN A THING
(IF IT AIN'T GOT THAT SWING)

Words by Irving Mills
Music by Duke Ellington

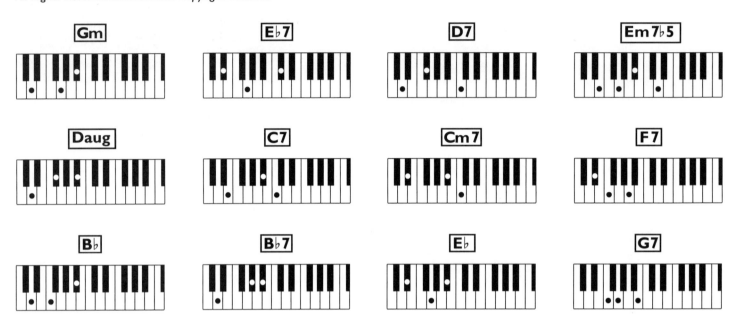

Voice: **Piano**

Rhythm: **Fox Trot**

Tempo: ♩ = 136

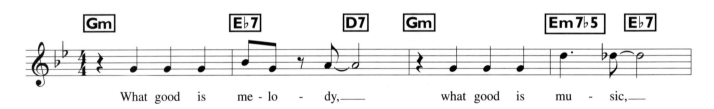

What good is me - lo - dy,___ what good is mu - sic,___

if it ain't pos - ses - sin' some - thing sweet?___

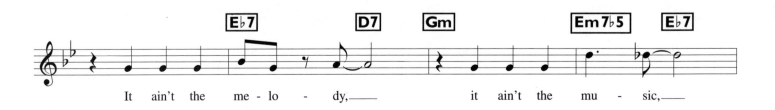

It ain't the me - lo - dy,___ it ain't the mu - sic,___

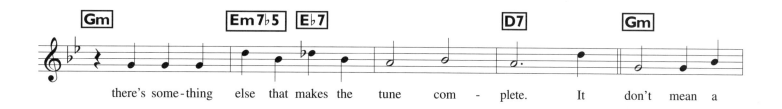

there's some-thing else that makes the tune com - plete. It don't mean a

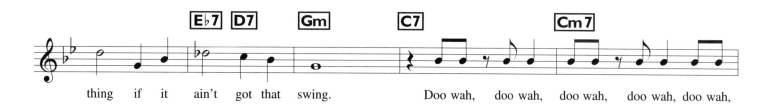

thing if it ain't got that swing. Doo wah, doo wah, doo wah, doo wah, doo wah,

doo wah, doo wah, doo wah, it don't mean a thing, all you got to do is

sing. Doo wah, doo wah, doo wah, doo wah, doo wah, doo wah, doo wah, doo wah. It

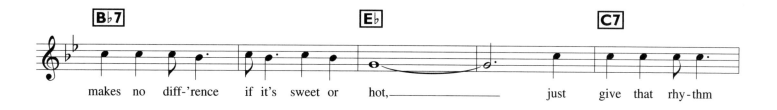

makes no diff-'rence if it's sweet or hot,_____ just give that rhy-thm

ev - 'ry-thing you got, oh. It don't mean a thing if it ain't got that

swing. Doo wah, doo wah, doo wah, doo wah, doo wah, doo wah, doo wah, doo wah.

JUMP, JIVE AN' WAIL

Words & Music by Louis Prima

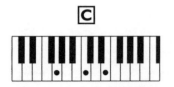
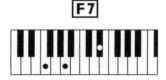

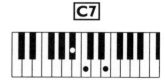

Voice: **String Piano Split**

Rhythm: **Swing**

Tempo: ♩ = 138

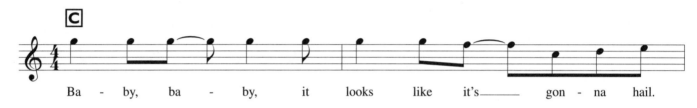

Ba - by, ba - by, it looks like it's ___ gon - na hail.

Ba - by, ba - by, it

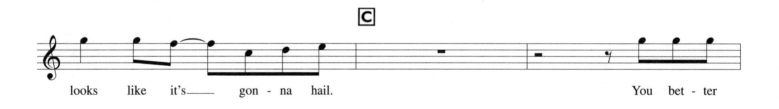

looks like it's ___ gon - na hail. You bet - ter

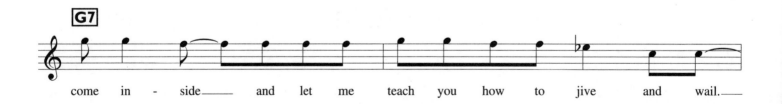

come in - side ___ and let me teach you how to jive and wail. ___

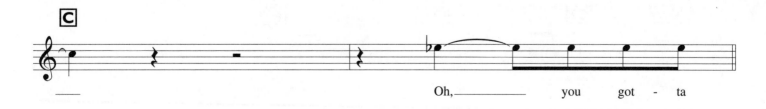

___ Oh, ___ you got - ta

Jump,——— jive and then you wail, you got - ta

jump,——— jive and then you wail. You got - ta

jump,——— jive and then you wail, you got - ta

jump,——— jive and then you wail, you got - ta

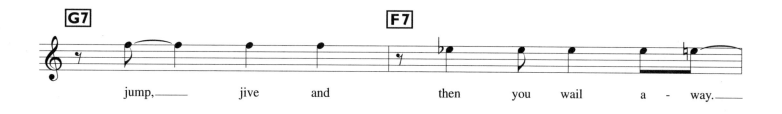

jump,——— jive and then you wail a - way.———

LAZY RIVER

Words & Music by Hoagy Carmichael & Sidney Arodin
© Copyright 1931 (renewed 1958) Peer International Corporation, USA.
Peermusic (UK) Limited, 8-14 Verulam Street, London WC1.

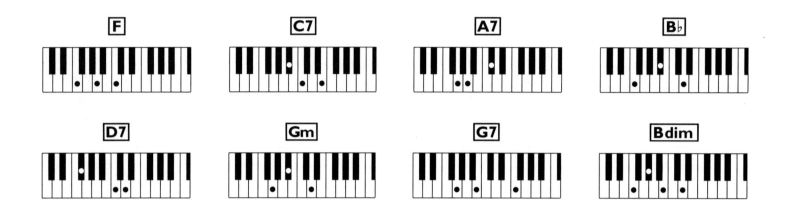

Voice: **Alto Saxophone**

Rhythm: **Swing**

Tempo: ♩ = 92

I like la - zy wea - ther,____ I like la - zy days,

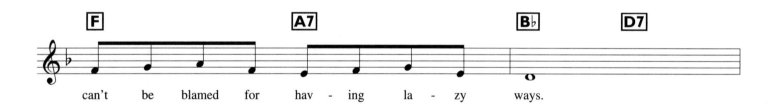

can't be blamed for hav - ing la - zy ways.

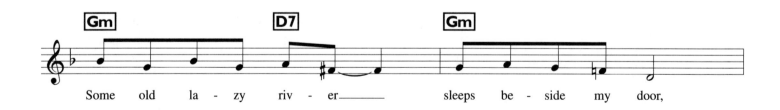

Some old la - zy riv - er____ sleeps be - side my door,

whis - p'ring to the sun - lit shore.

Up a la - zy riv - er by the old mill - run, that la - zy, la - zy riv - er in the

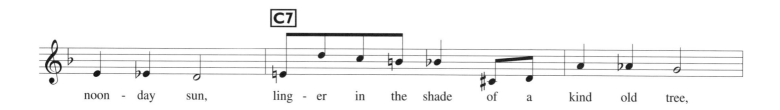

noon - day sun, ling - er in the shade of a kind old tree,

throw a - way your trou - bles, dream a dream with me.

Up a la - zy riv - er where the ro - bin's song a -

- wakes a bright new morn - ing, we can loaf a - long

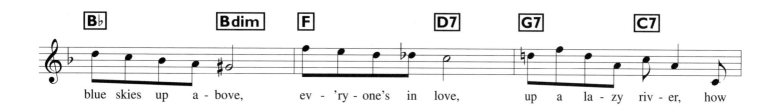

blue skies up a - bove, ev - 'ry - one's in love, up a la - zy riv - er, how

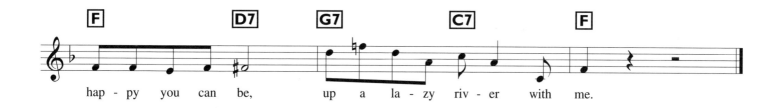

hap - py you can be, up a la - zy riv - er with me.

MOONLIGHT SERENADE

Words by Mitchell Parish
Music by Glenn Miller

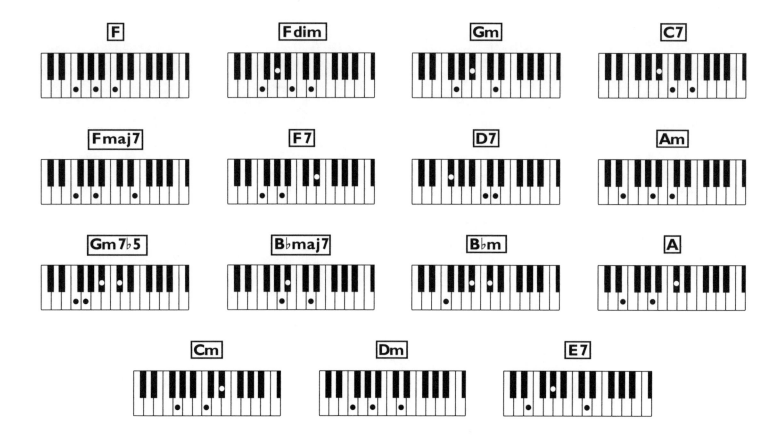

Voice: **Clarinet**

Rhythm: **Fox Trot**

Tempo: ♩ = 84

I stand___ at your gate___ and the song___ that I sing___ is of moon-light. I stand___ and I wait___ for the touch___ of your hand___ in the

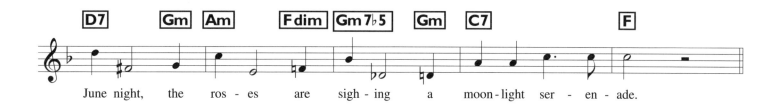

June night, the ros - es are sigh - ing a moon - light ser - en - ade.

Let us stray till break of day in love's val - ley of

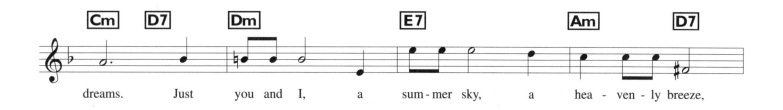

dreams. Just you and I, a sum - mer sky, a hea - ven - ly breeze,

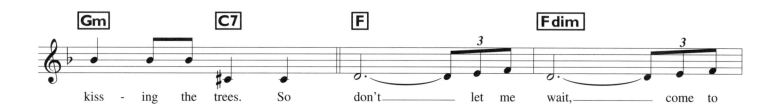

kiss - ing the trees. So don't let me wait, come to

me ten - der - ly in the June night. I stand at your

gate and I sing you a song in the moon - light, a

love song, my dar - ling, a moon - light se - re - nade.

OH YES, TAKE ANOTHER GUESS

Words & Music by Al Sherman, Charles Newman & Murray Mencher

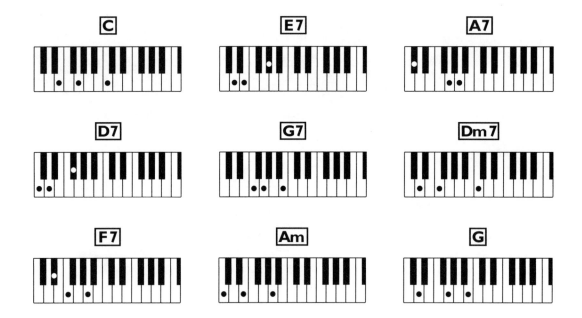

Voice: **Voice Ooh**

Rhythm: **Swing**

Tempo: ♩= 128

So you think I'll sit a - round and cry_____ the

day you say_____ "too - dle oo, good - bye!"_____ Oh yes?_____

_____ Take an - oth - er guess?   So you think no one can

fill your shoes____ and when you're gone,____ then I'll sing the blues,____ oh

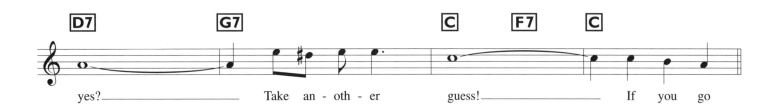

yes?_____ Take an - oth - er guess!_____ If you go

your way_____ then I'll go my way._____

____ And if you do____ as well as I do,____

ho - ney you'll do O. K._____ So you think I'll die of

lone - li - ness____ and the deep blue sea____ is my next ad - dress,____ oh

yes?_____ Take an - oth - er look._____

PERDIDO

Words by Harry Lenk and Ervin Drake
Music by Juan Tizol

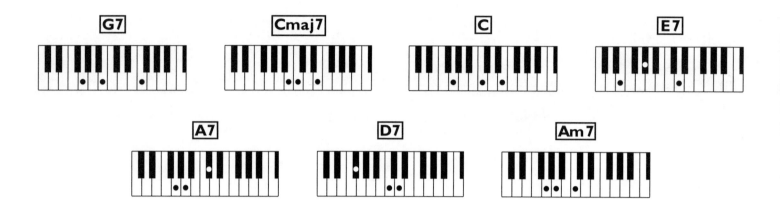

Voice: **Marimba**

Rhythm: **Cha-cha**

Tempo: ♩ = 128

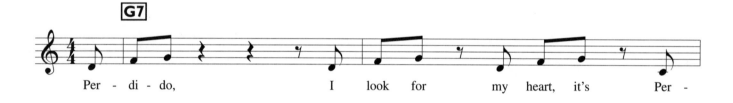

Per - di - do, I look for my heart, it's Per -

- di - do, I lost it way down in Tor - ri - do. The

day the fi - es - ta start - ed. Bo -

- le - ro, I swayed as they played a bo - le - ro, I

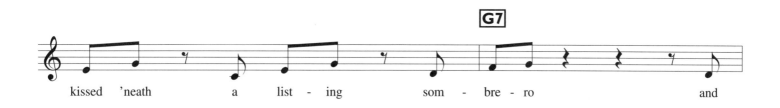

kissed 'neath a list - ing som - bre - ro and

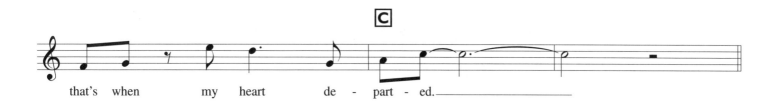

that's when my heart de - part - ed.____

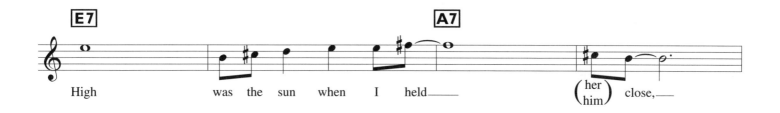

High was the sun when I held____ (her/him) close,____

low was the moon when we said____ "a - dios."____ Per -

- di - do, my heart ev - er since is Per - di - do, I

know I must go to Tor - ri - do to

find what I lost, Per - di - do.____

REET, PETITE AND GONE

Words & Music by Louis Jordan & Spencer Lee

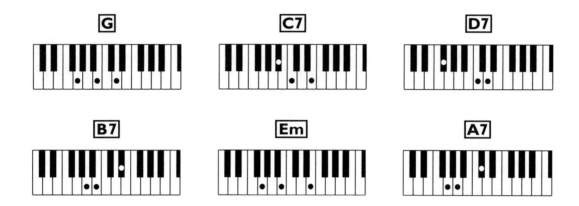

Voice: **Tenor Saxophone**

Rhythm: **Big Band**

Tempo: ♩ = 132

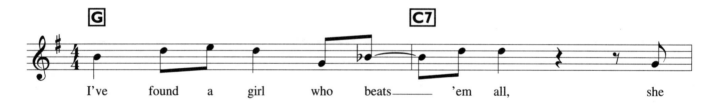

I've found a girl who beats 'em all, she

is-n't too short and she is-n't too tall, she's in the groove and right

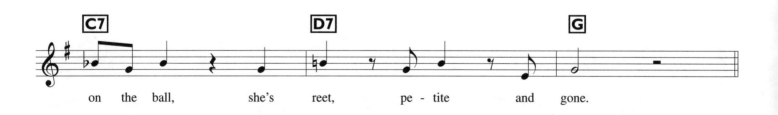

on the ball, she's reet, pe-tite and gone.

What a babe, she's the tops, when we go out they don't

need no traf - fic cops. One look at her___ and the traf - fic stops, 'cause she's

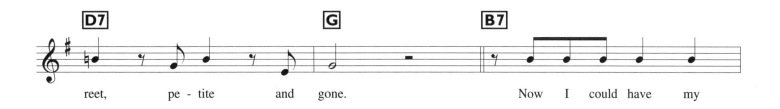

reet, pe - tite and gone. Now I could have my

pick you know, 'cause I got dough that's rea - dy to go,___

but this chick's so might - y fine, she got me all tied up like a

ball of twine.___ When I do things I do 'em right,

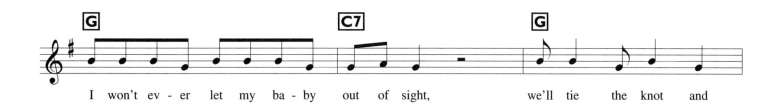

I won't ev - er let my ba - by out of sight, we'll tie the knot and

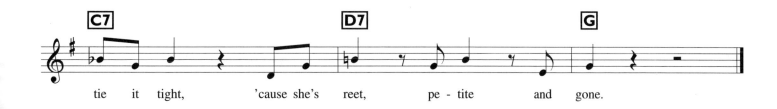

tie it tight, 'cause she's reet, pe - tite and gone.

SWING THAT MUSIC

Words & Music by Louis Armstrong & Horace Gerlach

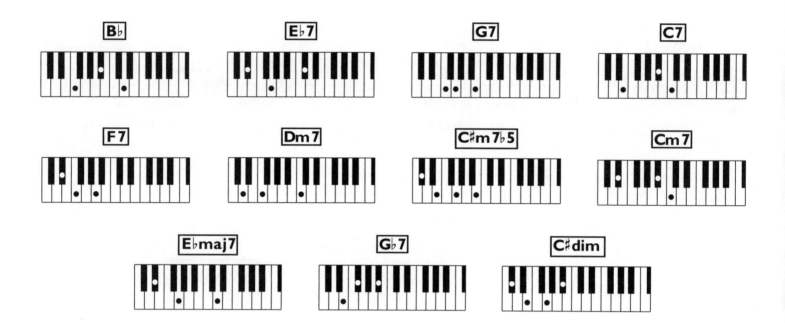

Voice: **Clarinet**

Rhythm: **Big Band**

Tempo: ♩ = 116

My heart gets a chill,_____ I feel such a thrill,_____

_____ my feet won't keep still_____ when they

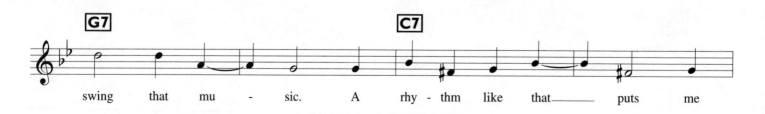

swing that mu - sic. A rhy - thm like that_____ puts me

TAIN'T WHAT YOU DO
(IT'S THE WAY THAT CHA DO IT)

Words & Music by Sy Oliver & James Young

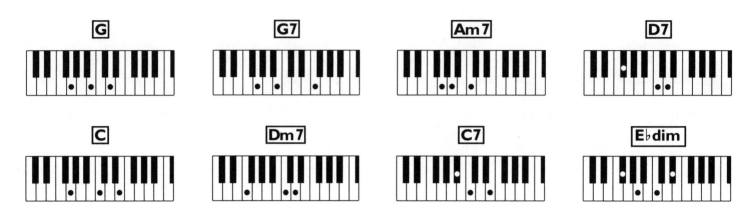

Voice: **Marimba**

Rhythm: **Swing**

Tempo: ♩ = 134

'Tain't   what   you   do,   it's   the   way   that   cha   do   it,

'tain't   what   you   do,   it's   the   way   that   cha   do   it,   'tain't   what   you   do,   it's   the

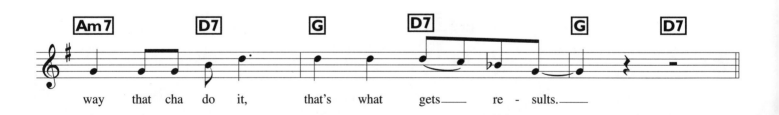

way   that   cha   do   it,   that's   what   gets____   re - sults.____

'Tain't   what   you   say,   it's   the   way   that   cha   say   it,   'tain't   what   you   say,   it's   the

TAKE THE 'A' TRAIN

Words & Music by Billy Strayhorn
© Copyright 1941 Tempo Music Incorporated, USA.
Campbell Connelly & Company Limited, 8/9 Frith Street, London W1.
All Rights Reserved. International Copyright Secured.

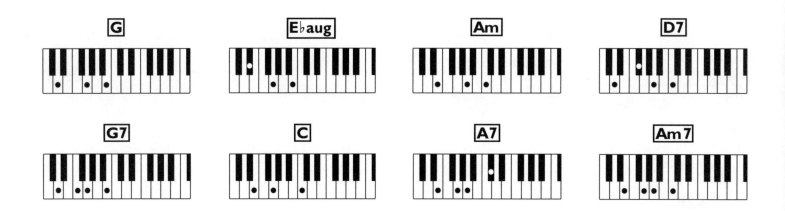

Voice: **Saxophone**

Rhythm: **Cool**

Tempo: ♩ = 108

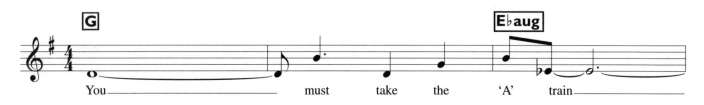

You _____ must take the 'A' train _____

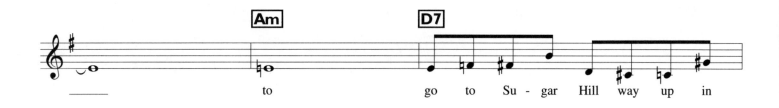

___ to go to Su - gar Hill way up in

Har - lem. _____ If _____

___ you miss the 'A' train, _____

you'll find you've missed the quick - est way to

Har - lem. Hur - ry,

get on now it's com - ing.

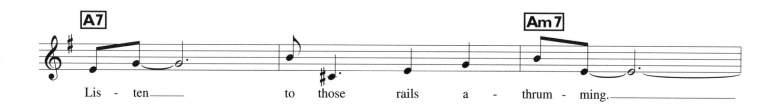

Lis - ten to those rails a - thrum - ming.

All 'board! get on the

'A' train. Soon

you will be on Su - gar Hill in Har - lem.

THE JOINT IS JUMPIN'

Words by Andy Razaf & J.C. Johnson
Music by Thomas "Fats" Waller

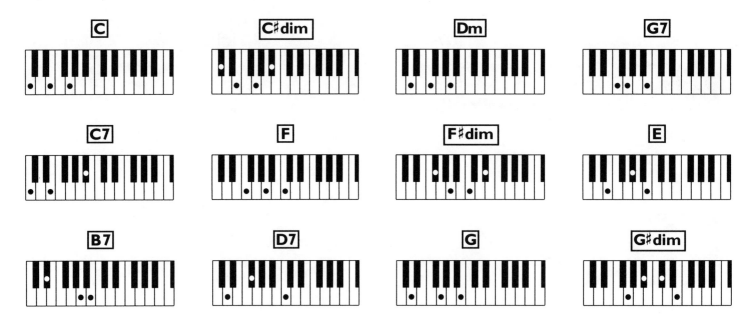

Voice: **Trumpet**
Rhythm: **Swing**
Tempo: ♩ = 136

This joint is jump-in', it's real-ly jump-in',

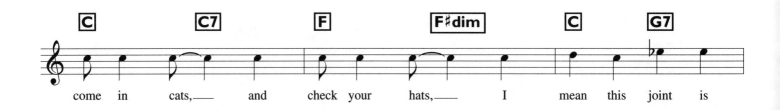

come in cats,— and check your hats,— I mean this joint is

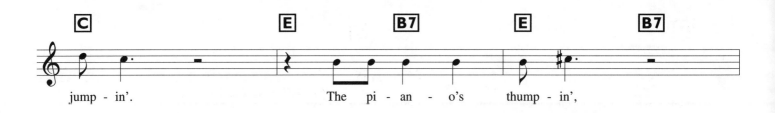

jump-in'. The pi-an-o's thump-in',

the dan - cers bump - in' this here spot___ is

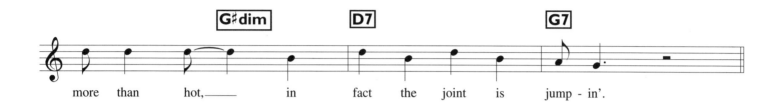

more than hot,___ in fact the joint is jump - in'.

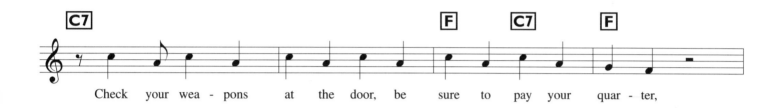

Check your wea - pons at the door, be sure to pay your quar - ter,

burn your wea - ther on the floor,___ grab a - ny - bo - dy's

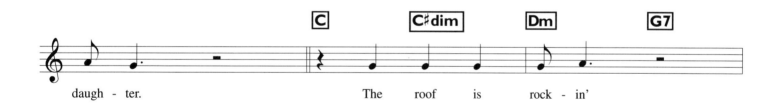

daugh - ter. The roof is rock - in'

the neigh - bours' knock - in', we're all bums when the

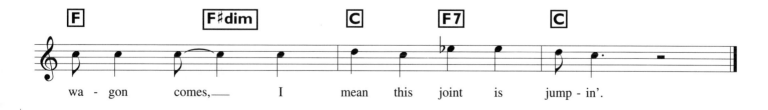

wa - gon comes,___ I mean this joint is jump - in'.

WATCH THE BIRDIE

Words by Don Raye
Music by Gene Paul

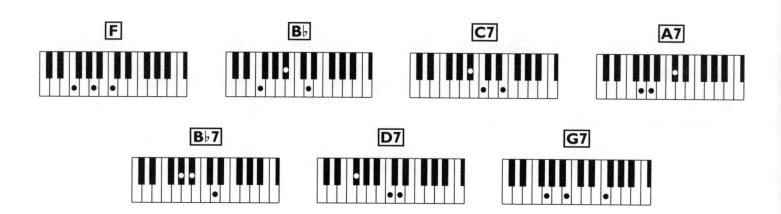

Voice: **Soprano Saxophone**

Rhythm: **Big Band**

Tempo: ♩ = 124

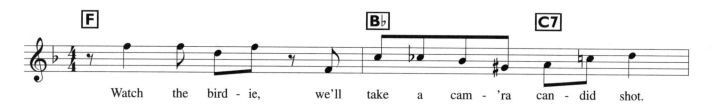

Watch the bird-ie, we'll take a cam-'ra can-did shot.

Watch the bird-ie, come on and give it all you got. Watch the bird-ie, just

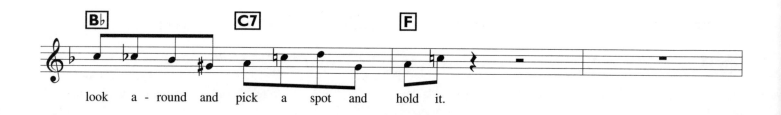

look a-round and pick a spot and hold it.

Watch the bird-ie, just strike a fun-ny pose a while. Watch the bird-ie, aw

you can beat that pose a mile. Watch the bird - ie, now let me see a pret - ty smile and

hold it. We're look - ing for a tall, dark

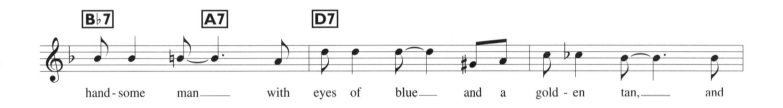

hand - some man with eyes of blue and a gold - en tan, and

strong white teeth like Joel Mc - Crae, hey you, will you get

out of the way. Watch the bird - ie, we'll take a cam - 'ra can - did shot,

watch the bird - ie, come on and give it all you got. Watch the bird - ie just

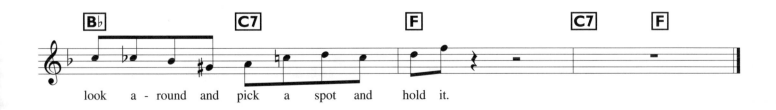

look a - round and pick a spot and hold it.

ZOOT SUIT RIOT

Words & Music by Steve Perry

Voice: **Jazz Guitar**

Rhythm: **Swing**

Tempo: ♩ = 140

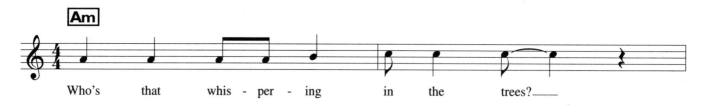

Who's that whis - per - ing in the trees?____

It's two sail - ors and they're on leave.____

Pipes and chains and swing - in' hands,____

who's your dad - dy? Yes I am.____

Fat cat came to play____ now____ he

can't   run   fast   e - nough._____

You'd   best   stay   a - - way_____   when   the

push - ers   come_____   to   shove._____

Zoot   suit   ri - ot   (ri - ot!)

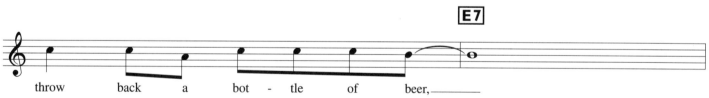

throw   back   a   bot - tle   of   beer,_____

zoot   suit   ri - ot,   (ri - ot!_____)   pull   a

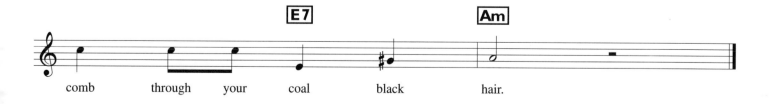

comb   through   your   coal   black   hair.

EASIEST KEYBOARD COLLECTION

Easy-to-play melody line arrangements for all keyboards with chord symbols and lyrics. Suggested registration, rhythm and tempo are included for each song together with keyboard diagrams showing left-hand chord voicings used.

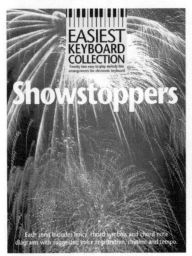

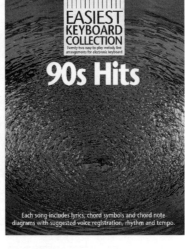

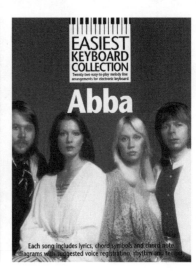

Showstoppers

Consider Yourself (Oliver!), Do You Hear The People Sing? (Les Misérables), I Know Him So Well (Chess), Maria (West Side Story), Smoke Gets In Your Eyes (Roberta) and 17 more big stage hits.
Order No. AM944218

Pop Classics

A Whiter Shade Of Pale (Procol Harum), Bridge Over Troubled Water (Simon & Garfunkel), Crocodile Rock (Elton John) and 19 more classic hit songs, including Hey Jude (The Beatles), Imagine (John Lennon), and Massachusetts (The Bee Gees).
Order No. AM944196

90s Hits

Over 20 of the greatest hits of the 1990s, including Always (Bon Jovi), Fields Of Gold (Sting), Have I Told You Lately (Rod Stewart), One Sweet Day (Mariah Carey), Say You'll Be There (Spice Girls), and Wonderwall (Oasis).
Order No. AM944229

Abba

A great collection of 22 Abba hit songs. Includes: Dancing Queen, Fernando, I Have A Dream, Mamma Mia, Super Trouper, Take A Chance On Me, Thank You For The Music, The Winner Takes It All, and Waterloo.
Order No. AM959860

Also available...

Ballads, Order No. AM952116	**The Corrs**, Order No. AM959849
The Beatles, Order No. NO90686	**Elton John**, Order No. AM958320
Boyzone, Order No. AM958331	**Film Themes**, Order No. AM952050
Broadway, Order No. AM952127	**Hits of the 90s,** Order No. AM955780
Celine Dion, Order No. AM959850	**Jazz Classics**, Order No. AM952061
Chart Hits, Order No. AM952083	**Love Songs**, Order No. AM950708
Christmas, Order No. AM952105	**Pop Hits**, Order No. AM952072
Classic Blues, Order No. AM950697	**60s Hits**, Order No. AM955768
Classics, Order No. AM952094	**80s Hits**, Order No. AM955779

...plus many more!